A Highly Subjective History of the 1990s

Kit Peacock

AUTHOR'S NOTE

This book was written for my daughter to tell her what life was like when I was growing up. If anyone else gets any good from it, I'm happy to have obliged.

As one person's recollections, I have also made this an **exercise in historiography**, i.e. in thinking about the biases of the writer when you use a source. This is a very useful skill in a world in which information, especially AI-produced, may be unreliable. I have purposely avoided checking facts too heavily beyond making sure in places that it was the 90s and not the 00s. In the back are some questions to get you started on this if you have never done it before.

I did ask a friend of similar age to proof-read the account (many thanks to JL for this) to make sure I hadn't written anything too controversial and have made the odd note where our recollections disagree.

A

Action Man – A muscular plastic doll about the size of a Barbie which usually came with an adventure theme, tools and accessories. Usually considered a boys' toy.

Advent Calendars – Usually only paper, chocolate or candles. The 'gift a day' type wasn't widely done.

Aerobics tape – If you wanted to exercise at home (gym going was not as common in the 90s as now) you could get a video, usually of a group of women standing in a row of neon suits doing exercises, to talk you through it.

Amazon – invented but a lot of people didn't have the internet; see Internet, Mail Order and Books.

American Adventure – A theme park in the midlands with a general wild west theme. It closed in the mid-00s but for years afterwards you could still see traces of it through the fence.

Animal toys – 90s animal toys and figures tended to have smaller heads and eyes than the ones now. You can see this if you compare a 90s Beanie Baby with a modern Beanie Boo.

Argos Catalogue – A huge catalogue of home items and toys. When making out birthday or Christmas lists, many children would go through the catalogue and circle the things they wanted.

Art on kids tv – There were many shows with step-by-step art skills, including Art Attack, Bitza, and various shows featuring Tony Hart.

Autism and ADHD – In the 90s, these were not well understood, and were thought to be almost exclusively male conditions. This is why we now have so many adults (especially women) in the 20s getting a late diagnosis.

Avocados – I don't remember ever being offered avocado to eat as a child. I suspect they didn't keep well in transport.

B

Baby All-Gone – a baby doll that pretended to eat cherries. It smelled amazing.

Barbie – plastic fashion doll steadily popular through the 90s as it had been in previous and subsequent years. Not as much variety in shape and appearance as in the 20s, but came in a couple of skin and hair colours. There were also Barbie films and computer games. Barbie had a boyfriend called Ken. There was a popular Barbie Girl pop song which was rather rude. See also Action Man.

Beanie Babies – soft toys filled with beans. Thought to be highly collectible, people kept the tags on them to keep their value. Most have not turned out to be valuable 30 years on.

Bees and wasps – You saw a lot more of them in the 90s than you do now.

Blair, Tony – Prime minister starting 1997 (Labour). Famous for the saying "Education, education, education". See School and University

Blue Peter – Children's TV show. I believe it is still on in the 20s, but it was much bigger in the 90s when we had fewer channels. It had a performance of some sort in each show, and a step-by-step art project. It had 'appeals' where you had to collect and send in a specific item for recycling e.g. bottle tops, aluminium cans, or money, which was then used to support a charity.

You could also get a Blue Peter Badge which got you free into various places and were considered a high honour – you can still get them today if you're over five.

Bob the Builder – Children's TV show and pop artist. If you want to see a really good example of the difference between girls in cartoons between the 90s and the 10s/20s watch both old and new Bob.

Bodger and Badger – Children's TV show in which a man was pelted with mashed potato by a badger puppet for some reason.

Book Token – A piece of paper the size of a bank note that was often sent as a gift to children. You could then use it only to buy books. Similar to the plastic gift cards you can buy now, except it was much harder to get change from a book token.

Books – Many poor families did not own any books at all, but better off people could access them easily via bookstores or mail order. Libraries were free. Audiobooks existed on CD and cassette tape and were free to borrow if you were visually impaired. The technology was there for e-books, but they didn't really take off until the 00s.

Collectible/vintage books were much harder to find in the 90s. You would usually have had to go to second hand bookshops and search.

Booster seats – Only babies and toddlers had to sit in a car seat. Older kids could sit either in the big seat or on a big polystyrene cushion called a 'booster seat'.

Bottled water – I can remember my father saying this would never take off, but it did. I also remember being told that it was rude to drink out of a bottle without a straw, but that may have just been us.

Brum – a kids TV show about a yellow car with eyes.

Bulldogs – a children's game where kids ran from one side of the playground to the other while people in the middle (the 'bulldogs') tried to catch them. It was banned in most schools because it caused a lot of injuries.

Bus – Our village had one bus service that went to the nearest town every twenty minutes. The service is exactly the same thirty years on, except the buses are now low emissions and the fare a lot higher.

Butterfly hair clips – small plastic hair clips that were shaped like butterflies, secured with a pincer movement.

C

Cabbage Patch Dolls – Soft baby-sized dolls with a large round head. Very popular.

Cadbury 99 ice cream – actually cost 99p at some point during the 90s.

Calculator – Usually solar powered small rectangular gadget used for doing simple maths. Children of the 90s were told that they must learn mental maths as they would not always have a calculator in their pocket. This prediction was wrong.

Caning in school – already outlawed in state schools. Technically still legal in independent schools in the 90s, but not at all widely used to my knowledge.
(Proof-reader tells me that teachers used to throw the blackboard eraser at children even after caning was banned).

Cars – Ran mostly on fossil fuels. Electric vehicles had been invented but they were used mostly for slow moving local vehicles, like milk floats. See Leaded Petrol.

Cassette tape – A way of playing music or stories on demand (see also CD below). They were a small rectangular plastic box with two wheels inside and a tape ran between the two wheels. If you turned the cassette over you could listen to more music on the other side. You had to wind them forwards and backwards to get to other parts of the music or story. They were more reliable than CDs because they didn't get scratched and they didn't jump if you bumped your gadget. However in the rare instance that the tape came out, it could get stuck in your gadget and make a big mess, if you weren't quick to wind it back in with a biro.

Cat (computer game) – An incredibly difficult game in MS Dos where you controlled a cat through various dangers – a big dog running across the bottom, people throwing things out of windows, etc. You could gain points by jumping through windows to do mini-games such as eating the goldfish, pushing a bird cage off the table, or putting dirt on the floor that was then cleared up by a broom. If you met a female cat you kissed it and the screen was full of hearts.

Cat's Cradle – A game with a large elastic band held between your hands. The object was to make a net that looked something like a cradle. Much older than the 90s.

Ceefax – Basic information that you could get on the television e.g. football results or weather forecasts.

Cereal Toys – in the 90s there was usually a plastic toy buried somewhere in the cereal. People considered these to be highly collectible, but they are not worth a great deal thirty years on. I'm not sure when the practice of doing this stopped.

Cheques – a piece of paper with a code carefully printed on the bottom that could be used to pay for goods and services. On the cheque you would write who it was to, the date, the amount of money in both numbers and words, and sign it at the bottom. You took the cheque to the bank and the bank would put the money in your account or give it to you in cash. This sometimes took a couple of days. Cheques still exist in the 20s but have been mostly taken over by cards and bank transfer.

Chocolate – a 'Freddo' cost 10p in the 90s. A standard size chocolate bar was between 30-40p, unless it was a particularly fancy one.

Christmas – widely celebrated both in the religious and secular community. Traditions included pantomimes, nativity plays and carol singing.
It was a smaller, cheaper affair in the 90s than it is now. 'Elf on the Shelf', matching pyjamas, and the 'Christmas Eve Box' were not common traditions in the UK until much later.
See also Advent calendars.
Other religions' holidays were celebrated but did not get as much public support.

Clocks – Both digital and analogue were in use, but analogue clocks were in wider use than they are today and most people could read them.

Clothing — Most people wore shop bought clothes though you could buy clothing patterns to make your own. Girls and boys usually dressed according to gender stereotypes though there was some overlap e.g. girls could wear trousers. It was much more accepted for a girl to wear 'boys' clothes than the other way around. (see Gender).

If you look at photos of the 90s, you will usually see that preteen kids looked much less polished than they do at the same age now. I think we probably did dress 'younger' than some kids do now, but also those pictures usually come from film cameras rather than digital. See Photography.

Coco Pops — chocolate covered rice cereal. The advert used to be a cartoon story with a monkey before the law changed to stop sugary cereals being marketed at children. At one point they changed their name to Choco Krispies but this was so unpopular that it was reversed back again.

Coffee — fancy coffee did exist, but it wasn't as popular to get a takeaway coffee as it is in the 20s.

Comics — Popular British kids comics included the Beano, Dandy, Girl Talk, Mizz, Animals of Farthing Wood, and various 'build your own' kits. There was a human body one where you could put together a model with different organs each week. The Beano cost about

40p a week, which was not expensive even then. The model making kits were often comparatively expensive.

Compact Disc (CD) – Alternative to cassette tape (see above) CDs were more expensive than cassette tapes. You would usually buy CDs from a music shop e.g. Virgin. Later on you could burn music onto a CD. You could also get computer games on a CD, though Floppy Discs were also used for this.

Computers – Our primary school had one computer for the Infants classes, which did not have Windows. The senior classes had one Windows and two BBC Basic machines between all the students. At home we had a black and white computer and later a Windows computer.
Our secondary school had Apple Macs, but I don't remember doing anything on them except playing Lemmings. In my second year they replaced them all with Windows PCs.

Conkers – Probably a lot older than the 90s. Children's game where you collected the nuts from horse chestnut trees (they're not edible so wash your hands if you try this) called conkers. These had a hole drilled down the middle and were then attached to a string. Players took it in turns to try and break the other player's conker off its string. Some people tried tricks to harden their conker such as baking it or painting it with nail polish. Still played today I believe but some schools have banned it due to risk of eye injuries.

Crazy Golf Machine – A board game in which you had to flick a tiny golf ball into a variety of obstacles.

Credit/Debit cards – Invented but there was no chip and pin – you had to sign the card and then sign a receipt to prove it was your signature. Contactless payment was not in use.

Currency – We had decimal currency (pounds and pence, not shillings). The two-pound coin came in the late 90s. Most people used cash for small purchases, bank cards or cheques for bigger ones.

D

Dip – a rhyme used to decide whose turn it was to do something. Examples:

"Ip dip, sky blue, it is not you."

"Eeny Meeny Miny Mo, catch a fish by its toe, if is squeals let it go, eeny meeny miny mo, o u t spells out." (None of us knew why we used 'fish' at the time, since fish do not have toes, but it was to replace a racist word in the original rhyme)

"There's a party on the hill would you like to come? (yes) Bring your own cup and saucer and your own cream bun (can't afford it). Who is your true love? (name) Name will be there with his/her knickers in the air what colour do you think they'll be? (colour) (Spell out colour)."

Digimon – 'Digital monsters' TV series. Wasn't as popular as Pokémon. (My proof-reader tells me they had a crossover with Tamagotchi, which is in the T section)

Disability Awareness – Hit and miss. The need for wheelchair access was fairly well understood, and you might occasionally see a wheelchair user on television. You might find a hearing loop in a public building like a bank or a doctor's surgery. You might have been able to get leaflets in large print or braille in some places. Mental health and developmental differences such as

Autism and ADHD were not as well understood as they are in the 20s. People in the 90s were much less open about having mental health problems.

Children with SEN more than mild learning difficulties (e.g. dyslexia) were more likely to go to a special school than they are now. That change occurred gradually, I can't put a date on it.

Disney – Very popular film company as it still is today, but the films were mostly hand drawn animation in the 90s. If you were a rich kid, you had the Disney Channel, which was on pay tv, and or the Disney Pencil Box with multiple compartments. Otherwise you either had to go to the cinema or watch it on video. Disneyland Paris opened in 1993, before that you had to go to America or Japan.

(Proof-reader tells me that Disney videos used to be released only in waves so you couldn't buy them all the time. My parents used to tape them off the television.)

Divorce – Definitely legal in the 90s but I don't recall personally knowing many people who did it. Possibly it wasn't discussed in front of children. (Proof-reader experienced it first hand and confirms it was unusual).

Dobby On – a tag game. One person was 'it' and if they tagged you, you became 'it'. I think 'dobby' might have been a regional name for it as I've never heard it called that anywhere else.

Dobby Scarecrow – a tag game – one person would be

'it' and would chase the other children. If tagged, the children would have to stand with arms and legs stretched. To free them, another child would go between the legs or under the arms depending on rules variations. The game ended if It caught all the children at once.

Doctor Dreadful Food Maker – a toy for making jelly sweets in gruesome shapes. They were horrible and tasted of grape.

Drones – they were invented but you wouldn't have had one at home. Model planes were owned by a few people.

E

E, Mr – A computer game played on the BBC Basic computer. See Computers.

Easter – was celebrated but on a smaller scale.

Eating out – People ate out much less in the 90s than they do in the 20s.

Ed, Edd n Eddy – a late 90s cartoon series about three boys all called Edward. The only episode I remember is the one where they all get new clothes which are too stiff to move in.

Eggs – It was widely believed that all raw eggs contained salmonella. Battery farming where hens were kept in tiny cages to lay eggs through a hole in the bottom was legal.

E-mail – Invented but not widely used.

Emoji – We had these in the 90s but they would not have been the colourful icons of nowadays. Children used symbols in a text message and then turned the phone sideways, e.g. :)

Environmental concerns – See also recycling. People of the 90s were not as worried about the state of the planet as they are in the 20s, but there were various causes such as saving the whales, eliminating the flatworms (if you found one you were meant to post it somewhere), holes in the ozone layer, and reducing consumption of water and electricity. People were less worried about single use plastic, but I don't think they used anything like as much of it.

European Union – The EU allowed free trade and movement between member countries for living, studying and working. It was also used to make collaborative laws between countries on subjects like human rights, trading standards, and so on. The UK was a member of the EU back in the 90s but did not change currency to the Euro.

F

Facebook – Not invented in the 90s, see Social Media.

Fireman Sam – Children's TV series about a fire department in Wales. In the 90s this was done with stop-motion animation and puppets and models, rather than by computer.

Fitness trackers – not invented beyond a basic pedometer. If you wanted to go for a jog you just did it.

Floppy Disc – A computer disc that was held inside a flat black square about the size of a coaster. The black square was solid, the inside bit that was floppy. Could small store things like documents or very basic computer games. Overtaken by CDROMs at some point. (Proof-reader tells me that there were bigger ones that actually were floppy.)

Fluffy notebooks – very popular in the late 90s. They were about two inches tall with a fluffy cover on a keyring.

Football – Most boys would have played football in the 90s, and some girls but not as many. Women's football was rarely if ever broadcast on television or radio.

Fox Hunting – Legal in the 90s but it was becoming controversial. Usually a sport of upper class men, who rode on horses accompanied by hound dogs to chase and kill foxes. It was banned in the 00s.

French Skipping – playground game (more played by girls). Two children would stand with a large elastic band stretched around their legs. A third child would jump in and out of the middle of the band. Probably a lot older than the 90s.

Friendship bracelets – Fashionable in the 90s among girls. Usually braided by hand from coloured embroidery floss and traded with your friend.

Frosties – Before children's advertising of sugar cereals was banned there was a cartoon advert of Tony the Tiger, who said Frosties were 'Grrrrrreat!'

Frosty, Mr – A toy for making iced drinks shaped like a snowman. The iced drink was made in the snowman's belly. They were heavily advertised at Christmas.

Furby – A small fluffy robot toy that looked a bit like an owl. They could dance, pretend to eat your finger, burp, play hide and seek, and be petted. They 'learned' new words the older they grew. It was widely rumoured that you could teach them to swear but I never saw that actually happen.

G

Gak – A type of slime, though it wasn't especially sticky. I think you could use it to copy ink pictures but its main uses were squashing it, bouncing it, and making fart noises with it.

Gender – Toys and clothes were usually made differently for boys than girls though there was some overlap. A girl who liked things designed for boys was called a 'Tomboy'. It was easier for girls to like boys' things than the other way around.
Non-Binary people did exist in the 90s (the term then was 'genderqueer') but did not have the freedom to speak about it that we see now. See LGBT rights.

Generation Game, The – a TV show in which two members of a family did challenges to try and win prizes. Challenges included throwing a pot in a few minutes, acting in a play without practice, and so on. The winning family had to memorise all the prizes on the conveyer belt, which always included a cuddly toy.

Gluten free food – if you wanted gluten free bread or other products in the 90s you would need to get them from the chemist on prescription, rather than finding them in the supermarket.

Goldfish – Back in the 90s you were allowed to buy a goldfish and keep them in a bowl with no filter. You could also win them at the fair.

Google – founded in the 90s but not widely used until later (see Internet). If you wanted to look something up, you used a book or went to the library.

Groovy Chick – Cartoon pictures of girls used on a lot of 90s merch like duvets and accessories. If you were a fashionable 90s girl, you probably had something with Groovy Chick on. I can't show you a picture because it's copyrighted, but easy to find on search engines.

Group Chat – I suspect some of the more sophisticated mobile phones could have texted two people at once, but I don't recollect ever seeing it in action. Certainly in about 97-98 I can remember us having a 'phone tree' at Guide Camp, which was an agreement that if there was an emergency the first person would telephone the second, who would phone the third, and so on.

H

Halloween – was celebrated but a much more low key affair than in the 20s.

Holidays – If you didn't have the internet you usually went to a travel agent to book your holiday. There were several TV shows e.g. 'Holiday' and 'Wish you were Here' which would review various popular destinations. (Proof-reader says you could find holiday deals in newspapers and on Ceefax).

Home schooling – existed in the 90s as it always has, however you would have likely had to do without the internet. Some TV channels showed educational programs at night which you might record on video.

Home working – did exist in the 90s but most homes did not have the internet, which would have limited what you could have done there.

Hopscotch – Popular game where you hopped up and down a row of numbered squares. Much older than the 90s.

I

Indians (and Cowboys) – In the 90s it was considered okay for children to dress as a 'Red Indian', paint your face or do a 'war cry'. Nowadays considered racist, but I couldn't put a date on when precisely that changed.

Internet – We as a family did not have the internet at home in the 90s, but it was invented. It was extremely slow, often taking several minutes at a time to load a single page. Home internet had to go through your phone landline, and when you connected it made a strange screeching noise.

Ireland – During the 90s Northern Ireland was in a period known as 'The Troubles'. I must confess I recollect very little of this as my parents used to turn the television off whenever it was mentioned*, but I do remember that Irish people were often treated unkindly in England. There was a series of jokes about the Englishman, the Scotsman and the Irishman in which the Irishman was usually the butt, which would probably not be considered acceptable nowadays.

(*Someone once accused me of saying the Troubles did not exist when I tried to explain this. It's actually a good example for this book – just because I don't personally remember it, doesn't mean it didn't happen.)

J

Jelly Shoes – These were a translucent sandal shoe usually worn at the beach or in the garden, made of a thick jelly. They usually had a pattern on the soles. I don't remember them being particularly comfortable. Now superseded by crocs.

Julia Jekyll and Harriet Hyde – 90s tv show about a girl (Julia) who keeps turning into an enormous monster girl (Harriet) at inconvenient moments. Had a friend called Edward Knickers.

Justin Timberlake – Popular 90s pop singer.

K

Kitty In My Pocket – Series of plastic toy cats, highly collectible at the time. Also had a magazine and later a website.

K'nex – a plastic building toy with sticks that slotted into connectors.

Knitting doll – a tube-shaped wooden toy with four pins on top. You pulled the wool over the pins in turn to make a long woollen snake.

L

Landline phone – most people did not have mobile phones in the 90s, so if you wanted to call someone, they needed to be at home. The landline phone was connected with a cable. They were not very private, because you couldn't take them away to your room. They sometimes had answerphones but could not receive a text message.

Leaded petrol – A car fuel that was phased out because lead is poisonous. That's why petrol these days is known as 'Unleaded'.

Left-Handedness – was recognised in the 90s.

Lego – popular in the 90s though invented long before. The doors were only five blocks high instead of six, and the figures were mostly male, though you could get a female head with lipstick.

Lemmings – computer game in which little creatures fell out of a hole and marched aimlessly across the screen – if they came to an obstacle they would just walk right into it. You had to direct them safely to a nest losing as few as possible.

LGBT people's rights – It was legal to be gay or lesbian or trans, but dangerous to be open about it. They could not get married to someone the same sex and some jobs could refuse to employ them. They were often treated badly. They were not usually seen on television in serious roles. Drag acts however were popular entertainment in television and theatre for adults and children. Identities other than gay, lesbian, bisexual and transgender were not very well understood outside of the LGBT community.

Light bulbs – Had a filament (a thin wire) that went across the inside of the bulb that glowed. The bulbs broke often and would not infrequently blow the fuse at the same time. LED lights were invented but not much used for room lighting.

Line Dancing – A fashionable dance activity usually done in large groups standing in rows. The dance moved from side to side.

Love, Like or Hate – a children's game. One child was blindfolded and lead around the playground to other children where they had to declare if it was someone they loved, liked or hated. Usually ended in an argument.

Lunch – Everyone at my primary school had a packed lunch, usually sandwiches, but some schools had school dinners. There were fewer options for take out food.

M

Mad Cow Disease – proper name BSE but nobody called it that. Disease of cattle that can cause brain damage and death. There was a big outbreak of it which led to a ban on British Beef in many countries. Before BSE you could get Oxtail Soup, which my father used to enjoy, but I don't think they've made it since.

Mail order – if you wanted to buy something through the post you would get a catalogue, fill in a form, and send a cheque in the post. About a month later, your items would arrive.

Major, John – Prime minister at the start of the 90s (Conservative).

Marriage – Only a man and a woman could marry. Most children were born to married parents. Most married women took their husband's name, unless they were doctors.

Men's Rights – Men were generally at an advantage in the workplace. They were more likely to be promoted to a top job or paid more than women, and they tended to do less childcare and household duties. However, those men who wanted to take on a more traditionally female role – stay at home parent, nurse, etc – would have had a hard time of it. They would have faced not only ridicule but barriers in the law. A father could not share parental leave after having a baby with the mother, for example. Children were also far more likely to be given to their mother's custody in a divorce.

Millennium bug – It was widely believed that every gadget with a computer calendar inside was going to malfunction when the date changed from 1999 to 2000.

Mmmbop – A very popular song. I have absolutely no idea what it was about.

Mobile phone – invented but most people did not have one. Teens were just starting to get them when I started secondary school in the late 90s. My first mobile phone had two lines of black and white text, no colour screen, and could only store ten messages at a time. Most phones would not have had internet access.

Mousetrap – A board game where players build a giant machine to catch mice. The winner is the last mouse to stay out of the net.

N

Names – some popular children's names when I grew up included: Thomas, Jack, James, Oliver, Timothy, Samuel, Joshua, Michael, Edward, Christopher, Lucy/Lucinda, Emma/Emily, Eleanor, Elizabeth, Lauren, Rachel, Rebecca, Charlotte, Catherine/Katie, Sara, Laura, Sophie and Claire. (Nb. I grew up in a not very diverse rural area, there would have been more variety in the cities).

90s parents generally gave children full names on their birth certificate if they planned to use a nickname. It would have been unusual to have a child legally named 'Lizzie', for example, as opposed to 'Elizabeth'.

Most 90s kids were born to married parents and had the same last name as both parents, unless they were doctors, almost always the father's surname. Double-barrelled surnames were less common than now, and usually indicated unmarried parents or a blended family.

National Lottery, The – Six balls and a bonus ball were picked by a machine shaped like a gumball dispenser. The machines had names after the Camelot stories e.g. Lancelot. Started during the 90s and the first episode was a big deal. It came with a big show including a psychic (Mystic Meg) and a musical act. Gradually faded into the background over the years that followed. Tickets cost £1 at the time.

Neon – bright neon clothes and accessories were very fashionable in the 90s. Who wouldn't want to be dressed like a traffic cone while dancing at the disco?!

News – most people got their news from the radio, television or newspaper rather than the internet. You could get rolling news (Sky, BBC 24) on pay TV.

Newspapers – Many people had a newspaper delivered every day to their house, usually by a 'paper boy' (or girl). A lot of newspapers, such as The Times, were printed on 'broadsheet' paper, which was about twice as big as modern newspapers. Some newspapers had pictures of ladies wearing little or no clothes on the third page.

Nokia – Mobile phone owned by the cool kids. (NB the one considered coolest of all was the Nokia 3310, but that didn't come out until 2000)

Noel's House Party – a Saturday night TV show run by Noel Edmonds in the fictional village of Crinkly Bottom. He had a big pink monster with yellow spots called Mr Blobby, who said only "Blobby blobby blobby!". Every week he dunked a guest in the gunge tank.

NOW CDs – CD albums that collected the most popular songs of the year.

O

Opal Fruits – the old name for Starburst.

Oxtail Soup – see Mad Cow Disease.

P

Pets Win Prizes – a game show presented by Dale Winton where animals would compete in a series of intelligence tests e.g. a maze.

Phones – see Mobile Phones and Landline

Photography – Digital cameras were invented in the 90s but most people would have had a colour film camera. You bought a film from the chemist, and in a dark room (if the film got into the light you lost all your pictures), put it into the camera. When you took a photo, the shutter lifted for a very short moment and the picture would be marked onto the film. Some cameras would wind the film on by themselves, others you had to turn a little wheel. You then took it back to the chemist at the end of the film, who 'developed' the film into pictures.

You would only get a small number of pictures on a film (24 I think) and there was usually no preview, which is why pictures from the 90s generally look terrible. Photo editing did exist to an extent, but a 90s film camera would not have had much in the way of filters. Most people did not have a camera in their phone. See also Selfies.

Pingu – Children's tv show with plasticine model penguin, famous for making a 'noot noot' noise when annoyed.

Playdays – General kids tv show with educational segments of video. It started off with a bus that would stop at different stops – the ones I remember were the Why Bird Stop and the Roundabout Stop. When I date checked this, Wikipedia said that there were other stops on different days of the week, which I don't remember. I suspect I was watching episodes taped off the tv (there's another source limitation for you, kids!).

Play-doh – was invented but my mother used to make ours out of flour, salt, oil and food colouring. It was rather slimy.

Pluto – was considered a planet, later downgraded to a dwarf planet.

Pogs – Circular cardboard discs that children collected. I think there was a way to play a game with them but I can't remember what it was.

Pokémon – 'Pocket monsters' Japanese cartoon, video game and card game. Massively popular in the late 90s.

Postman Pat – Children's cartoon – stop motion animation. In the 90s Pat delivered regular letters and parcels in a single post van.

Pound Puppies/Pound Purries – small collectable children's toy dogs/cats. Some were soft toys and some were tiny plastic ones. They were usually posed in a sort of splat shape.

Power Rangers – another very popular children's show. I wasn't allowed to watch it because my school banned it in the playground on fear of expulsion.

Princess Diana – First wife of the now King Charles III (Prince Charles at the time) and mother of Prince William and Prince Harry. She separated from Charles and was frequently seen in the press until her death in a car crash in 1997. There was very large-scale public mourning for Diana and a great many theories as to how her car crash happened were put forward.
As a child I can remember the Sunday morning cartoon channels were switched off while the news was announced over and over again on a background of sombre music.

Pronouns – (See LGBT people's rights) Gender neutral pronouns e.g. they/them were not in common use in the 90s.

Puppy in my Pocket – See Kitty in my Pocket – small plastic toy dogs, popular collectible.

Q

Queen Elizabeth II – the reigning monarch in the 90s.

Quinoa – It existed but I suspect most 90s people would not have heard of this, let alone eaten any.

R

Racism – We as kids had a rough idea that treating people badly for their skin colour was bad, but those of us from a white rural area knew very little more than that. At my primary school, when the first Asian kids joined, we had to have an assembly to explain racism because some of the kids had never met a non-white person before. We didn't know about concepts such as microaggressions, cultural misappropriation or racial stereotyping. We may have been behind city kids in this respect however.

Among adults there was also a lot of misunderstanding and suspicion of people who dressed differently, especially if they covered their head. Speaking a foreign language in public might make you a target of abuse. Laws to prevent institutional racism were not very developed, which lead later to various enquiries in health, policing, and other public services.

(NB – a much more accurate interpretation of this topic would be the recollection of someone on the receiving end).
See also White Privilege.

Radio – The channels were similar in the 90s to the ones on FM radio in the 20s, apart from minor name changes. Digital/internet radio had not really taken off. You could call the radio station to request a song. You could also record the radio onto a cassette tape to play again later.

Recycling – There was no household recycling bin when I was a little girl but I believe some areas did have limited collection according to their council. We took ours to public recycling bins at the supermarket, or to the tip. More of our waste is recyclable now than it was back then.

S

S Club 7 – Popular band among children, most famous song was 'Reach for the Stars'.

Scooby Doo – Children's TV show in which four teenagers and a dog solve mysteries. The 'monster' always turned out to be someone in a rubber mask, who would say 'I would have gotten away with it too if it weren't for you meddling kids'.

School – All children had to have schooling (either at school or home schooled) until age 16 by law. Most children took GCSE exams at 16. Some went on to do A levels or went to college, but you didn't have to by law. See University.

Selfies – not really a thing in the UK in the 90s, unless you wanted to look very silly. You could pack into a photo booth with friends though. Selfies didn't really take off until the invention of the front facing smart phone.

Shopping – most people went out to the shops to buy things. A few of the bigger shops – see Argos Catalogue – would print large colour page catalogues. Internet shopping had not taken off on a large scale but you could place orders by phone or mail. These were usually very slow to arrive.
I don't think supermarket home delivery was widely used in the 90s. However you could certainly have milk

delivered and I think the milkman brought a few other basic groceries.

Sindy – rival fashion doll to Barbie.

Slaps – A hand game played by two children. Put your hands together palm to palm sticking out in front of you. One person starts, they try to slap the other person's hands. The other person must try and lift their hands up at the same time as the slap occurs. If the person slapping misses, it is the other player's turn.

Smacked bottoms – legal but gradually going out of fashion.

Smart phones – almost nobody had a phone with internet access in the 90s. Google tells me that the Blackberry was invented by the late 90s, but I don't remember smart phones being in common usage until the mid to late 00s.

Smartboards – not invented. You either had a chalk board or a whiteboard with pens. They were usually on a loop and could be scrolled around to the other side. A favourite school prank was to draw a silly picture on the back of the board. If you were to watch a video in class the television was wheeled in on a trolley.

Smoking – Cigarette smoking was known to be harmful but it was still popular and it was legal in public places. Restaurants sometimes had a 'no smoking' area, but it was not uncommon to be sitting eating your lunch and have someone start smoking right next to you. The e-cigarette was not invented yet.

Snake (game) – One of the earliest mobile games – a black line (the snake) is directed around the screen. A black dot is somewhere else on the screen. The snake is directed to eat the dot and becomes longer. You lose the game if you crash the snake into its own tail. It was technically possible to have the snake fill the entire screen. Early versions were just a line, but later versions had better resolution and an actual snake head shape. Sounds simple but it was hugely popular at the time.

Social Media – invented to an extent but not nearly as widely used as it is in the 20s because few mobile phones had internet access.

Solar Power – invented but not as good as it is now. You were more likely to see it powering a dancing flower toy than a house.

Spice Girls – massively popular girl band famous for 'Girl Power'. They were nicknamed Posh Spice, Baby Spice, Sporty Spice, Scary Spice, and Ginger Spice. Biggest song was 'Wannabe'. Posh Spice (Victoria) went on to marry the footballer David Beckham.

Stamps – Postage stamps had Queen Elizabeth II's head on, unless it was a special stamp e.g. at Christmas. They didn't have a barcode. You had to lick the back to make it stick to the envelope.

Straws – these were usually made of plastic. Plastic straws were substantially better to drink with than paper ones, but it turned out that a lot of them ended up in the sea.

Steps – another great 90s band famous for the dance song 5,6,7, 8. See Line Dancing.

Streaming – the technology possibly existed but the internet was not fast enough in the 90s to do this.

Street lighting – unlike the lights most commonly seen now in the 20s, street lamps were usually a deep yellow colour, meaning that everything looked a strange colour when you were out at night. They ran on electricity.

Subbuteo – a tabletop football game with model footballers on round bottomed stands. There were lots of accessories that you could buy e.g. players of your favourite team. Players took turns to flick a player against a ball.

Sunny Delight – fashionable orange juice.

Sushi – invented but not as freely available in the 90s as it is in the 20s. You couldn't buy a sushi pack from the supermarket, you would have to go to a restaurant.

T

Tablet computers – not invented in the 90s. Touchscreens were notoriously unreliable and hard to use.

Takeaway food – existed but much less variety than now and fewer places did home delivery.

Tamagotchi – a pocket robotic pet. It needed attention all day for thirty or so days at a time to be fed, played with and medicated. They were so popular on first release that people queued for hours to get one.

Taxis – You could either go to a taxi rank or phone for one. Uber wasn't invented until much later. Your driver would not have had a GPS unit either, they would have to memorise the map in their heads.

Teletubbies – Children's tv show with four giant baby-like creatures with televisions in their bellies. Although they are still around in the 20s, when they first came along in the 90s, they got a lot more attention. The Tellytubby song reached number 1 in the UK for several weeks.

Television – a standard TV had four channels – BBC1, BBC2, ITV and Channel 4. Channel 5 was introduced in the late 90s. Children's television was on for a few hours in the mornings and afternoons. Additional channels could be purchased via a satellite dish or cable. Live streaming on the internet was impossible as the internet in the 90s was too slow.

You couldn't pause the television to go to the toilet, and if you missed a show it might never be on again! You could record on a video cassette (see video) but most people watched television live. Most people watched the same episode of a show at the same time, and had to wait until the next episode to be shown. Televisions were also a lot deeper in shape than the modern 'flat screen'.

Tetris – a computer game where four-block shapes fall from the top to the bottom of the screen. If you made a full line across the screen those blocks disappeared. The game got gradually faster and faster. When the blocks touched the top of the screen you lost the game.

Text messaging – Invented but a lot of people did not have a mobile phone. Messages cost 10p each on my first phone (though I didn't have that until the 00s) and the number of letters or numbers were limited so people often used abbreviations known as txtspk, eg gr8 instead of great. See Emoji.

Thomas the Tank Engine – Popular children's TV show with trains. The 90s version was stop motion animation (see Fireman Sam, Postman Pat).

Thumb War – a game played by two people. You put your hand up like a thumbs up, and wrapped your four fingers around your opponent's four fingers, leaving your thumb sticking up as if it is a little person. You start the game by tapping your thumbs from side to side and saying "One, two, three, four, I declare a thumb war. Bow (bow your thumb), kiss (put your thumb against opponents), begin!". You then try to trap your opponent's thumb before they catch yours, without letting go of the fingers. You have to catch it long enough to say "One, two, three, four, I win thumb war."

Tom and Jerry – a children's cartoon with a cat trying to catch a mouse. Some of the episodes were later criticised for racist stereotypes.

Top Sheets – A bedsheet that sat between your body and the duvet. These don't seem to be used any more though I'm not sure when that changed.

Toy Story – the first fully computer animated children's film. It was absolutely huge in the UK – up until that we watched mostly stop-motion animation (models) or hand drawn cartoons.

U

Um Bongo – a mixed fruit drink marketed at children. Not as popular now but apparently it does still exist. The song from the 90s advert is generally considered racist in the 20s.

Unicorns – not as widely popular in the 90s as they are in the 20s.

University – Fewer than half of school leavers went to university at the start of the 90s, and tuition was free. Tony Blair wanted half to go to university when he came to power in the late 90s, and you had to pay a tuition fee (though it was substantially less than the fees in the 20s are).

V

Vegetarianism/Veganism – A small percentage of people were vegetarian in the 90s. There were limited veggie options in cafes and supermarkets. Vegans did exist but they were rare. You would have had a much harder time being vegan in the 90s than you would now.

Video recorder – used video tapes or VHS (see cassette tapes) to record a particular channel at a particular time. They were notoriously unreliable because if the show started or ended a few minutes late you would lose the start or end of your program. Video tapes could be watched over and over, and you could record over them again. You had to wind them back to start the program again.

Video Shop – Films or video cassettes could be rented for a short time for a small fee e.g. £3.
(Proof-reader tells me that video shops got the latest releases before they could be purchased by the public, 3-6 months after release at the cinema.)

W

Walkman – a portable music player for cassette tapes or CDs. They usually had a radio also.

Wallace and Gromit – Film series about a plasticine man and his dog. The one that hit peak hype was The Wrong Trousers, though that's actually the second one.

Wheelie Shoes – Trainers with wheels in the heel went through a craze in the late 90s but I recall having a pair and only wearing them once because it was too difficult. Roller blades and roller skates were easier.

White Privilege – The UK was a majority white country in the 90s; as it still is, but it was much harder to be an ethnic minority person in the 90s (see racism). You were less likely to be given a top job if you were not white. You would be hard pressed to find things like tights for dark skinned people, but if you looked hard you might find a black baby doll.
In rural areas it was often especially hard. The primary school I went to had only two Indian children and one black child out of a hundred. There were cultural communities in the bigger cities though.
Representation in film and TV was gradually improving. You might see one black character in a children's TV show.

Women's Rights – Hot topic particularly in the late 90s (see Spice Girls) when 'Girl Power' was all the rage.

Many job titles were changing to gender neutral terms e.g. Police officer instead of Policeman. But women were nevertheless more disadvantaged in pay and opportunities than they are today and tended to do more childcare/household duties than men. You did not for example often see Dads at pickup in the school playground. Of course, there were exceptions. See Men's Rights.

X

X-men – existed in the 90s but more well known in the UK in the 00s onwards, as more American comics and tv became available and channels like Cartoon Network became more popular.

Y

Yo-yos – invented long before the 90s but went through a craze. I remember them having the ability to spin on the end of the string before you pulled them back up again. Popular tricks included 'walking the dog'. They often came with glowing lights which lit up when you played with it.

Yu-gi-oh – Japanese manga, anime and trading card game. Not as big in the UK as Pokemon.

Z

Zoos – Not as animal-friendly in the 90s as they are in the 20s, zoos were more focused on letting people see the animals than giving the animals the best enrichment.

QUESTIONS TO THINK ABOUT

1. What are the limitations of this source? Is it reliable to get your facts from one person?

2. How do you think an author's age, gender and social class might affect their recollections of the past?

3. Which do you think is more accurate: a child's diary written at the time, or an adult's memories written with more understanding of the bigger picture?

4. Where could you look for a more reliable source?

5. How do you think the introduction of AI software will affect the reliability of history you find online?

Printed in Great Britain
by Amazon

21608597R00038